**Quick Start Guides**

CW00385779

The Essential
SOUP
Recipe Book

100 Delicious & Nutritious Soup Recipes

Easy Soup Making Cookbook

First published in 2020 by Erin Rose Publishing

Text and illustration copyright © 2020 Erin Rose Publishing

Design: Julie Anson

ISBN: 978-1-9161523-9-7

A CIP record for this book is available from the British Library.

DISCLAIMER: This book is for informational purposes only and not intended as a substitute for the medical advice, diagnosis or treatment of a physician or qualified healthcare provider. The reader should consult a physician before undertaking a new health care regime and in all matters relating to his/her health, and particularly with respect to any symptoms that may require diagnosis or medical attention.

While every care has been taken in compiling the recipes for this book we cannot accept responsibility for any problems which arise as a result of preparing one of the recipes. The author and publisher disclaim responsibility for any adverse effects that may arise from the use or application of the recipes in this book. Some of the recipes in this book include nuts. If you have a nut allergy it's important to avoid these.

CONTENTS

The Ultimate Health and Weight Loss Food

Soups are a delicious and convenient way of eating foods which boosts your health and trims your waist-line!

Enjoying a bowl of warm, nourishing soup is not just comforting, it's packed with good ingredients which are filling and make you feel good from the inside out.

- Soup helps you lose weight while feeling full.

- It gives you plenty of wholesome goodness when you are ill or under the weather.

- It's warming, hydrating and satisfying.

- It's a great way of feeding children hidden vegetables.

- It freezes and re-heats well.

- It tastes great!

Soup is the ultimate skinny food, containing low-calorie vegetables, fibre, vitamins, minerals and a wide variety of essential nutrients.

Soup is pure liquid nutrition and it's easy to digest. You'll need fewer calories if you start a meal with soup, as you'll feel satisfied with less food. Nutrient-dense soups make you feel satiated, nourished and fuelled with vitality while trimming your waist line.

Soup is one of the best ways to boost your immune system, hydrate, warm your body and fend off colds and flus.

Soups can be quick to make, easy to store and handy for batch cooking, ready for lunches or dinners when you don't have much time to spare.

The recipes in this book are not only easy and delicious, they are calorie-counted too! So, if you wish to keep track you can, and you'll know you're fuelling your body in the best possible way. You can enjoy tasty home-made soups for all occasions, whether you want a flavoursome lunch, a quick wholesome dinner, a light meal to curb your appetite, or you want to support your whole body health and lose weight.

This book provides you with plenty of delicious recipes; spicy soups, comforting broths, pasta and noodle soups or refreshing summer soups. You'll find meals the whole family can enjoy. You can add your favourite bread, make delicious croutons and toppings too. You can multiply the recipes and batch cook your favourites for weekday meals and lunches on the go. You can blend vegetables to a purée and add them to that the popular kid's favourite tomato soup or Mediterranean Meatball soup which is a winner.

Many of the recipes contain easy-to-find ingredients, store cupboard essentials, plus renowned healthy ingredients like olive oil, herbs, spices, avocados, pulses, fresh and frozen vegetables found in the best healthiest all-round diets.

Here's to good soup, great health and vitality!

Mediterranean Tomato & Lentil Soup

SERVES 4

156 calories per serving

Ingredients

400g (14oz) tin of chopped tomatoes

350g (12oz) tinned cooked lentils (drained)

1 onion, peeled and chopped

1 teaspoon tomato purée (paste)

1 teaspoon dried mixed herbs

1 tablespoon olive oil

900mls (1½ pints) hot vegetable stock (broth)

A large handful of fresh basil leaves, chopped

Sea salt

Freshly ground black pepper

Method

Heat the oil in a frying pan, add the onion and cook for 4 minutes. Add in the vegetable stock (broth), tomatoes, lentils and dried mixed herbs and bring them to the boil. Simmer for around 5 minutes. Stir in the basil. Use a food processor or hand blender and process until smooth. Season with salt and pepper. Serve and enjoy.

French Onion Soup & Gruyère Croutons

Ingredients

100g (3½ oz) Gruyère cheese, grated (shredded)

6 onions, peeled and finely sliced

4 slices baguette

3 cloves of garlic, crushed

750mls (1¼ pints) hot chicken stock (broth)

2 tablespoons olive oil

2 tablespoons Worcestershire sauce

Pinch salt

Freshly ground black pepper

SERVES 4

322 calories per serving

Method

Place the oil, onions, garlic, Worcestershire sauce, stock (broth), salt and pepper into a slow cooker and stir the mixture really well. Cook on a low heat for around 4 hours. When ready to serve, place the bread slices under a hot grill (broiler) and toast it on one side. Turn it over and sprinkle some cheese on top then return it to the grill until the cheese has melted. Serve the cheese crouton on top of the soup and eat straight away.

Chunky Chicken & Vegetable Soup

**SERVES
6**

250
calories
per serving

Ingredients

4 carrots, peeled and roughly chopped

4 celery stalks (including leaves) roughly chopped

2 leeks, roughly chopped

1 whole small chicken

1 onion, peeled and chopped

2 sprigs fresh thyme

2 garlic cloves, chopped

1 handful of fresh parsley, chopped

2.5 litres (approx. 5 pints) chicken stock (broth)

Method

Quarter the chicken into two leg portions and two breast portions and remove any excess fat from the tail and neck. Place all of the chicken in a large saucepan and add the stock (broth). Bring it to the boil, reduce the heat and simmer for 20 minutes. Using a slotted spoon, skim off any excess grease from the surface of the liquid. Now you can add in the onion, garlic, carrots, celery, leeks and thyme. Simmer gently for 1½ hours or until the chicken has completely cooked. Remove the chicken carcass and once again skim off any fat which has floated to the surface. Stir in the chopped parsley. Serve into bowls.

Thai Chicken Soup

Ingredients

200g (7oz) cooked chicken, chopped

2 teaspoons fresh coriander (cilantro), chopped

1 teaspoon ground ginger

1 teaspoon thai red curry paste

1 red pepper (bell pepper), chopped

100mls (3½ fl oz) coconut milk

400mls (14fl oz) chicken stock (broth)

2 teaspoons olive oil

SERVES 2

297
calories
per serving

Method

Heat the olive oil in a frying pan, add the red pepper (bell pepper) and cook for 3 minutes. Pour in the stock (broth), ginger and add the curry paste. Cook for 1 minute. Pour in the coconut milk and stir in the chicken. Cook for 10-15 minutes. Sprinkle in the coriander (cilantro) and serve.

Beef & Mushroom Soup

Ingredients

100g (3½ oz) cooked sliced beef, chopped

4 large mushrooms, finely sliced

6 spring onions (scallions), finely chopped

2 sticks of celery, finely chopped

2 teaspoons olive oil

600mls (1 pint) beef stock (broth)

Sea salt

Freshly ground black pepper

**SERVES
2**

133
calories
per serving

Method

Heat the oil in a saucepan, add the mushrooms, spring onions (scallions), celery and cook for 3-4 minutes. Pour in the stock (broth) and chopped beef. Bring it to the boil, reduce the heat and cook for 10 minutes. Season with salt and pepper. Serve and enjoy.

Lentil & Bacon Soup

Ingredients

- 400g (14oz) tin chopped tomatoes
- 200g (7oz) lentils
- 6 rashers of smoked streaky bacon, chopped
- 2 carrots, peeled and finely chopped
- 1 onion, peeled and finely chopped
- 1.5 litres (2½ pints) vegetable stock (broth)
- 2 tablespoons chopped fresh parsley
- 1 tablespoon olive oil

SERVES 4

302 calories per serving

Method

Heat the olive oil in a saucepan. Add the bacon, onion, carrots and cook over a medium heat, stirring occasionally for 8-10 minutes, or until the bacon has started to turn golden and the vegetables have softened. Add the lentils to the pan and stir well. Add the chopped tomatoes and stock (broth). Bring to the boil, cover, and then simmer the soup gently for about 1 hour, or until the lentils are tender. Sprinkle in the parsley and serve.

Mexican Bean Soup & Tortilla Croutons

Ingredients

400g (14oz) tinned chopped tomatoes

250g (8oz) cooked black beans, drained and rinsed

50g (2oz) feta, sliced thinly

2 corn tortilla wraps

1 red onion, peeled and diced

1 red pepper (bell pepper), deseeded and chopped

1 yellow pepper (bell pepper), deseeded and chopped

1 tablespoon Mexican tinga paste

1 clove of garlic, finely chopped

½ avocado, chopped

600mls (1 pint) hot vegetable stock (broth)

2 tablespoons olive oil

A small handful fresh coriander (cilantro), chopped

SERVES 4

350 calories per serving

Method

Heat a tablespoon of oil in a large saucepan. Add the peppers and onion and cook for 5 minutes. Add the garlic and Mexican tinga paste and cook for 1 minute. Add in the beans, tomatoes and stock (broth). Bring it to the boil, reduce the heat and simmer for 10 minutes. In the meantime, heat a tablespoon of oil in a frying pan. Cook the tortillas, for 1 minute on each side. Remove them and once they have cooled slightly, cut them into triangles. Serve the soup into bowls. Scatter some avocado, feta, and coriander (cilantro) on top and add the tortilla triangles.

Egg Drop Soup

Ingredients

250mls (8fl oz) chicken stock (broth)

1 teaspoon butter

1 egg

1/4 teaspoon chopped garlic

Pinch of chilli flakes

Sea salt

SERVES 1

120 calories per serving

Method

Heat the butter and chicken stock (broth) in a saucepan and bring it to the boil. Add in the garlic, chilli and salt and stir. Remove it from the heat. In a bowl, whisk the egg then pour it into the saucepan. Stir for around 2 minutes until the egg is cooked. Serve and eat immediately.

Tomato & Pepper Soup With Cucumber Raita

Ingredients

400g (14oz) tinned chopped tomatoes

3 red peppers, (bell peppers), deseeded and chopped

3 cloves of garlic, chopped

2 onions, peeled and chopped

1 carrot, peeled and chopped

1 red chilli, sliced

900mls (1½ pints) vegetable stock (broth)

1 tablespoon olive oil

FOR THE CUCUMBER RAITA
4 tablespoons plain natural yogurt (unflavoured)

½ cucumber, deseeded and grated

A small handful of fresh mint leaves, chopped

SERVES 4

191 calories per serving

Method

Heat the oil in a large saucepan. Add in the carrot, onions and red peppers (bell peppers). Cook for 10 minutes then add the garlic, chilli, chopped tomatoes and stock (broth). Bring to the boil, reduce the heat and simmer for 15 minutes or until the vegetables are completely cooked. In the meantime, in a small bowl, combine the yogurt, mint and cucumber. Using a food processor or hand blender, blitz the soup until smooth. You can add a little extra stock (broth) or hot water if you need to thin the soup a little. Season with salt and pepper. Serve the soup into bowls and add a dollop of the minty yogurt mixture.

Creamy Vegetable Soup

Ingredients

300g (11oz) crème fraîche

175g (6oz) Cheddar cheese, grated (shredded)

25g (1oz) cream cheese (full fat)

2 carrots, peeled and grated (shredded)

1 medium head of broccoli, cut into florets

1 onion, peeled and chopped

2 cloves of garlic, chopped

1 teaspoon dried mixed herbs

450mls (15 fl oz) chicken stock (broth)

Sea salt

Freshly ground black pepper

SERVES 4

312 calories per serving

Method

Place the carrots, onion, broccoli, cream cheese, stock (broth), garlic and herbs into a slow cooker and mix well. Cook on a low heat for around 4 hours or on high for 2-3 hours. Stir in the crème fraîche. Transfer half of the soup to a deep bowl and using a hand blender, process it until it is smooth. Return the mixture to the slow cooker and stir it in thoroughly. Warm the soup further if you need to. Season with salt and pepper. Serve it into bowls with a sprinkling of cheese on top. Enjoy.

Spicy Chicken & Chickpea Soup

Ingredients

450g (1lb) chicken fillets, cut into chunks

400g (14oz) tinned chopped tomatoes

275g (10oz) tinned chickpeas, drained

2 cloves of garlic, crushed

2 tablespoons fresh coriander (cilantro) leaves, chopped

1 red pepper (bell pepper), de-seeded and chopped

1 onion, peeled and chopped

1 teaspoon paprika

1 teaspoon ground cumin

1 teaspoon Harissa paste

750mls (1¼ pints) chicken stock (broth)

SERVES 4

308 calories per serving

Method

Place the chicken into a slow cooker and add in the vegetables. Pour in the stock (broth) and stir in the garlic, spices and Harissa paste. Cook the soup on a low heat for 8 hours or on high for around 5 hours. Sprinkle in the fresh coriander and stir. Serve on its own or with a dollop of plain (unflavoured) yogurt.

Seafood Chowder

Ingredients

450g (1lb) cod fillets, roughly chopped

400g (14oz) tin of chopped tomatoes

275g (10oz) potatoes, peeled and diced

25g (1oz) butter, melted

3 tablespoons plain flour (all-purpose flour)

2 stalks of celery, finely chopped

2 teaspoons dried parsley

1 onion, peeled and chopped

1 carrot, peeled and finely diced

1 teaspoon salt

1 teaspoon white pepper

600mls (1 pint) fish or vegetable stock (broth)

50mls (2fl oz) double cream (heavy cream)

Splash of tabasco sauce

SERVES 4

338 calories per serving

Method

Place the fish, potatoes, onion, celery and carrot into a slow cooker. Sprinkle in the salt, pepper, parsley, tomatoes and a splash of tabasco sauce. Pour in the stock (broth) and stir all the ingredients well. Cook on a low heat for 7 hours or on high for 3 hours. In a small bowl, mix together the butter, cream and flour until it becomes smooth then slowly add the mixture to the soup, stirring continuously. Cook for 40 minutes. Serve into bowls and enjoy.

Curried Carrot Soup & Cashew Salsa

Ingredients

1200g (2³/₄ lb) carrots, peeled and chopped

8 green cardamom pods

5cm (2.5 inch) chunk of fresh ginger, chopped

4 tomatoes, chopped

3 onions, finely chopped

2 teaspoons garam masala

2 teaspoons cumin seeds

2 teaspoons coriander seeds

2 green chillies, chopped

1 teaspoon turmeric

1 teaspoon fenugreek

2 litres (4 pints) vegetable stock (broth)

200mls (7fl oz) coconut milk

1 tablespoon olive oil

Juice of 1 lemon

FOR THE CASHEW SALSA:

150g (5oz) cashew nuts, finely chopped

4 spring onions (scallions), finely chopped

A large handful of fresh coriander (cilantro), finely chopped

SERVES 6

357 calories per serving

Method

Heat the olive oil in a saucepan. Add the coriander seeds, cumin seeds and cardamom pods and cook until they begin to pop. Add in the onion and carrot and cook for 5 minutes. Add in the tomatoes, fenugreek, turmeric, chilli, ginger garam masala and cook for 10 minutes, stirring occasionally. Add the vegetable stock (broth), bring it to the boil, reduce the heat and simmer for 30 minutes. Using a food processor or hand blender, blitz the soup until smooth. Add in the lemon juice and season with salt and pepper. Pour in the coconut milk and warm it through. In a small bowl, combine the ingredients for the salsa. Serve the soup into bowls and add some cashew salsa on top.

Smoked Haddock & Potato Soup

SERVES 4

413
calories
per serving

Ingredients

300g (11oz) smoked haddock fillet, skin removed

200g (7oz) new potatoes, peeled and chopped

25g (1oz) butter

1 onion, peeled and chopped

400mls (14fl oz) chicken stock (broth)

100mls (3½fl oz) milk

200mls (7fl oz) double cream

Method

Heat the butter in a large pan, add the onion and cook it gently for 5 minutes. Add the potatoes and cook for another 5 minutes. In a separate pan, pour in the milk and cream and bring it to a simmer. Add the haddock fillet and cook it for 3-4 minutes until it is just cooked through. Using a fork, break the haddock into flakes. Using a food processor or hand blender, blitz the soup until smooth and creamy. Stir in the haddock and milk mixture. Season with salt and pepper. Warm the soup completely before serving into bowls. Enjoy straight away.

Pea Soup

Ingredients

450g (1lb) frozen peas

3 tablespoons crème fraîche

1 leek, washed and chopped

1 onion, peeled and chopped

1 stalk of celery, finely chopped

1 small handful of fresh mint leaves, chopped

750mls (1¼ pints) vegetable stock (broth)

Sea salt

Freshly ground black pepper

**SERVES
4**

131
calories
per serving

Method

Place the onion, leek, celery and peas into a slow cooker and pour on the stock (broth). Cook on high for 3-4 hours or on low for 5-6 hours. Stir in the chopped mint and let it cook for 10 minutes. Season with salt and pepper. Using a hand blender, blitz the soup until smooth. Stir in the crème fraîche. Serve and eat straight away.

Creamy Celeriac Soup

SERVES 6

113 calories per serving

Ingredients

2 onions, peeled and chopped

1 head of celeriac, peeled and chopped

1 potato, peeled and chopped

1 clove of garlic, chopped

1 teaspoon dried parsley

750mls (1¼ pints) hot vegetable stock (broth)

Sea salt

Freshly ground black pepper

2 tablespoons crème fraîche

Method

Place all of the vegetables into a slow cooker and pour on the vegetable stock (broth) and add the garlic and dried parsley. Cook on low for 6 hours or on high for around 3 hours. Using a hand blender, process the soup until smooth. Season with salt and pepper then stir in the crème fraîche. Serve and eat immediately.

Carrot, Coriander & Butterbean Soup

Ingredients

400g (14oz) butter beans
4 carrots, peeled and chopped
1 onion, peeled and chopped
1 courgette (zucchini), chopped
1 clove of garlic, chopped
900mls (1½ pints) vegetable stock (broth)
1 handful of fresh coriander (cilantro), chopped
Sea salt
Freshly ground black pepper

**SERVES
4**

159
calories
per serving

Method

Heat the vegetable stock (broth) in a large saucepan. Add in all of the vegetables except the coriander and butterbeans. Bring them to the boil, reduce the heat and simmer for 20 minutes. Add the butterbeans and stir until warmed through. Add in half of the chopped coriander (cilantro). Using a hand blender or food processor, process the soup until smooth. Sprinkle with the remaining coriander and serve.

Turkey & Chickpea Soup

Ingredients

300g (11oz) cooked turkey (leftovers are ideal), cut into strips

200g (6oz) tinned chickpeas (garbanzo beans), drained

1 onion, peeled and chopped

1 red pepper (bell pepper), de-seeded and chopped

2 teaspoons ground coriander (cilantro)

2 teaspoons butter

1 handful of fresh parsley, chopped

1½ litres (2½ pints) vegetable stock (broth)

Sea salt

Freshly ground black pepper

SERVES 4

234 calories per serving

Method

Heat the butter in a large saucepan, add the onion and cook for 2 minutes. Add in the red pepper (bell pepper), ground coriander (cilantro) and stock (broth). Bring it to the boil, reduce the heat and simmer for around 6 minutes. Stir in the turkey, chickpeas (garbanzo beans) and parsley and warm it through. Season with salt and pepper. Serve into bowls and enjoy.

Spanish Chorizo & Peppers

**SERVES
6**

448
calories
per serving

Ingredients

500g (1lb 2oz) chorizo sausage, cut into slices

150g (5oz) tomato purée (paste)

6 cloves of garlic, chopped

2 green peppers (bell peppers), deseeded and chopped

2 red onions, peeled and chopped

2 litres (4 pints) vegetable stock (broth)

1 teaspoon white wine vinegar

Method

Scatter the sausage into a slow cooker; add the peppers, garlic, onion, tomato purée, vinegar and stock (broth). Stir it well. Cook on a low heat for 7 hours. This can be served on its own as a side dish or with vegetables, rice or potatoes.

Fennel & Bean Soup

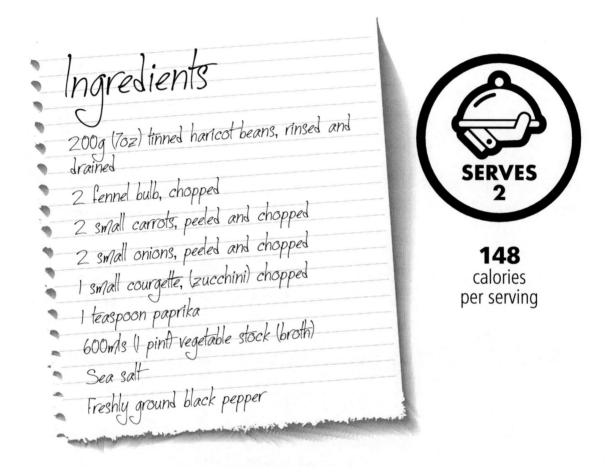

Ingredients

200g (7oz) tinned haricot beans, rinsed and drained

2 fennel bulb, chopped

2 small carrots, peeled and chopped

2 small onions, peeled and chopped

1 small courgette, (zucchini) chopped

1 teaspoon paprika

600mls (1 pint) vegetable stock (broth)

Sea salt

Freshly ground black pepper

SERVES 2

148 calories per serving

Method

Place all of the ingredients, except the beans, salt and pepper, into a saucepan and bring it to the boil. Reduce the heat and simmer for 20 minutes. Add the haricot beans to the saucepan and warm them for 5 minutes. Season with salt and pepper and serve. If you want to have a smooth soup, simply blitz it using a hand blender or food processor before adding the beans.

Tomato & Pesto Soup

Ingredients

6 tomatoes, roughly chopped

4 teaspoons crème fraîche

2 stalks of celery, chopped

2 teaspoon pesto sauce

600mls (1 pint) hot stock (broth)

Sea salt

Freshly ground black pepper

SERVES 2

81 calories per serving

Method

Place the tomatoes, celery and pesto into a saucepan and add the water and stock (broth). Cook for 8-10 minutes. Using a hand blender or food processor blitz the soup until it's smooth. Add the crème fraîche and stir well. Season with salt and pepper then serve.

Chicken & Asparagus Soup

SERVES 2

235
calories
per serving

Ingredients

4 asparagus stalks, finely chopped

2 chicken breasts, finely chopped

2 carrots, finely diced

1 courgette (zucchini), finely chopped

600mls (1 pint) chicken stock (broth)

1 teaspoon lemon juice

2 teaspoons olive oil

Freshly ground black pepper

Method

Heat the olive oil in a saucepan, add the chicken and cook it for 5 minutes, stirring occasionally. Pour in the stock (broth) and add the courgette (zucchini), lemon juice, carrot and asparagus. Bring it to the boil, reduce the heat and simmer for 15 minutes. Season and serve.

Poached Eggs With Pea & Lettuce Soup

Ingredients

400g (14oz) frozen petit pois

15g (approx. ½ oz) butter

4 eggs

3 shallots, finely sliced

3 cloves of garlic, sliced

1 large round lettuce, chopped

900mls (1½ pints) vegetable stock (broth)

1 tablespoon olive oil

A small handful fresh mint leaves

A small handful fresh dill

**SERVES
4**

216
calories
per serving

Method

Heat the butter in a large saucepan. Add the shallots and garlic and cook for 5 minutes. Add in the lettuce and cook for around 2 minutes, stirring occasionally. Add in the peas, stock (broth) and mint. Bring to the boil, reduce the heat and simmer for 10 minutes. Using a food processor or hand blender, blitz the soup until smooth.In the meantime, bring a saucepan of water to a simmer. Stir it with a spoon to create a whirlpool. As the water begins to settle, crack an egg into the middle of the saucepan. Cook for around 2-3 depending on how well you like the eggs cooked. Repeat for all the eggs. Remove them and set them aside. Ladle the soup into bowls and top it off with a sprinkling of dill and a poached egg. Divide the soup between 4 bowls. Top each one with a poached egg and some dill.

Quick Green Gazpacho Soup

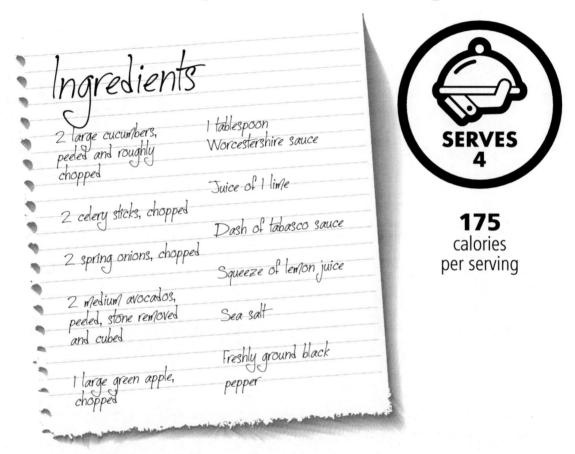

Ingredients

2 large cucumbers, peeled and roughly chopped

2 celery sticks, chopped

2 spring onions, chopped

2 medium avocados, peeled, stone removed and cubed

1 large green apple, chopped

1 tablespoon Worcestershire sauce

Juice of 1 lime

Dash of tabasco sauce

Squeeze of lemon juice

Sea salt

Freshly ground black pepper

SERVES 4

175 calories per serving

Method

Place the cucumbers, celery, apple, spring onions, avocado and lime into a food processor and process and blitz until smooth. Add in a squeeze of lemon juice, Worcestershire sauce, tabasco and stir well. Season with salt and pepper. Serve chilled and you can add a few ice cubes if you wish.

Creamy Leek & Ham Soup

Ingredients

4 slices of ham, finely chopped

2 small leeks, chopped

2 cloves of garlic, chopped

2 tablespoons fresh parsley, chopped

2 tablespoons crème fraîche

2 teaspoons butter

1 onion, peeled and chopped

600mls (1 pint) vegetable stock (broth)

Sea salt

Freshly ground black pepper

SERVES 2

165
calories
per serving

Method

Heat the butter in a saucepan, add the leeks and garlic and cook for 5 minutes until they have softened. Add in the stock (broth). Bring it to the boil, reduce the heat and simmer for 15 minutes. Stir in the parsley and crème fraîche. Using a food processor or hand blender, process the soup until smooth and creamy. Season with salt and pepper. Stir in the ham and serve into bowls.

Hot & Sour Chicken Soup

Ingredients

450g (1lb) chicken breast fillets, sliced

200g (7oz of tinned bamboo shoots, drained and finely sliced

150g (5oz) Oyster or shitake mushrooms

150g (5oz) chestnut mushrooms, sliced

100g (3 ½ oz) Chinese leaf, shredded

2.5cm (1inch) chunk of fresh ginger root, peeled and grated

3 tablespoons cornflour (cornstarch) mixed with 4 tablespoons of cold water

1 clove of garlic, crushed

1 red chilli, finely chopped

1 spring onion, sliced

1 small handful of coriander, roughly chopped

900mls (1½ pints) hot vegetable stock

2 tablespoons dry sherry

2 tablespoons light soy sauce

1 tablespoon rice vinegar

1 tablespoon groundnut oil

1 lime, quartered for garnish

SERVES 4

271 calories per serving

Method

Heat a large wok or frying pan over a high heat and add the groundnut oil. Add in the chicken and fry it for around 5 minutes or until pale golden. Add in the ginger, garlic, and chilli and stir-fry for a few seconds. Add the Chinese leaf and mushrooms and stir fry for 1 minute. Add the stock (broth), bamboo shoots, dry sherry, vinegar, soy and cornflour (cornstarch) mixture. Bring it to the boil and simmer for 1 minute. Remove it from the heat and garnish with coriander (cilantro) and spring onion. Serve with a wedge of lime.

Creamy Tomato Soup

Ingredients

2 x 400g (14oz) tins of chopped tomatoes

25g (1oz) butter

2 tablespoons parsley, minced, optional

1 red onion, chopped

600mls (1 pint) vegetable stock (broth)

150mls (5fl oz) double cream (heavy cream)

Sea salt

Freshly ground black pepper

**SERVES
4**

293
calories
per serving

Method

Heat the butter in a saucepan, add the onion and cook for 5 minutes. Add in the tomatoes and stock (broth) and bring it to the boil. Reduce the heat and simmer for 5 minutes. Using a food processor and or hand blender blitz until smooth. Pour in the cream and warm it. Sprinkle in the parsley and season with salt and pepper. Serve straight away.

Green Vegetable Soup

Ingredients

- 450g (1lb) broccoli, chopped
- 1 large leek, chopped
- 1 fennel bulb, chopped
- 1 courgette (zucchini), chopped
- 1 handful parsley, chopped
- 1 handful chives, chopped
- Sea salt
- Freshly ground black pepper

SERVES 4

61 calories per serving

Method

Place the broccoli, leek, courgette (zucchini) and fennel in enough water to cover them and bring to the boil. Simmer for 10-15 minutes or until the vegetables are tender. Stir in the herbs. Using a hand blender or food processor blend until the soup becomes smooth. Add more water if required to adjust the consistency. Season and serve.

Chicken Curry Soup

Ingredients

- 450g (1lb) cooked chicken, shredded
- 75g (3oz) basmati rice
- 3 cloves of garlic, chopped
- 2.5cm (1 inch) chunk of fresh ginger, peeled and chopped
- 2 carrots, peeled and chopped
- 1 teaspoon cumin seeds
- 1 teaspoon mustard seeds
- 1 onion, peeled and chopped
- 1/2 swede, peeled and chopped
- 1 tablespoon mild curry powder
- 900mls (1½ pints) chicken stock (broth)
- 1 tablespoon olive oil
- Sea salt
- Freshly ground black pepper

SERVES 4

300 calories per serving

Method

Heat the olive oil in a large saucepan, add the cumin and mustard seeds and cook until they begin to pop. Add all of the vegetables and season with salt and pepper. Simmer for 15-20 minutes then add in the stock (broth), curry powder and shredded chicken. Simmer for 5 minutes. Add the rice and cook for 20 minutes or until the rice is cooked through. Season with salt and pepper. Serve into bowls and enjoy.

Mediterranean Potato Soup

Ingredients

400g (14oz) potatoes, diced

400g (14oz) tinned chopped tomatoes

150g (5oz) cabbage,

1 leek, chopped

900mls (1½ pints) vegetable stock (broth)

1 teaspoon fresh or dried oregano

Sea salt

Freshly ground black pepper

SERVES 4

117
calories
per serving

Method

Pour the stock (broth) into a large saucepan and add the leek, potatoes and tomatoes. Bring them to the boil, reduce the heat and simmer for 15 minutes. Add in the cabbage and oregano and simmer for a further 5 minutes. Season with salt and pepper and serve.

Cream of Asparagus Soup

Ingredients

900g (2lbs) asparagus spears

2 tablespoons crème fraîche

1 onion, chopped

1 tablespoon olive oil

900mls (1½ pints) chicken stock (broth)

Sea salt

Freshly ground black pepper

SERVES 4

104 calories per serving

Method

Heat the oil in a large saucepan, add the onion and cook for 5 minutes. Break off the tough root end of the asparagus and roughly chop it. Place it in the saucepan and add the stock (broth). Bring it to the boil, reduce the heat and simmer for 20 minutes Using a food processor or hand blender process the soup until smooth and creamy. Stir in the crème fraîche. Season and serve.

Cream Of Mushroom Soup

SERVES 4

126 calories per serving

Ingredients

450g (1lb) mushrooms, chopped

1 large leek, finely chopped

1 tablespoon cornflour (corn starch)

750mls (1¼ pints) vegetable stock (broth)

150mls (5fl oz) crème fraîche

1 tablespoon olive oil

Sea salt

Freshly ground black pepper

Method

Heat the olive oil in a saucepan. Add the leek and mushrooms and cook for 8 minutes or until the vegetables are soft. Sprinkle in the cornflour (corn starch) and stir. Pour in the stock (broth), bring it to the boil and simmer for 20 minutes. Stir in the crème fraîche. Using a hand blender or food processor, blend the soup until smooth. Return to the heat if necessary. Season with salt and pepper just before serving.

Creamy Chicken & Vegetable Soup

Ingredients

275g (10z) leftover roast chicken (or other cooked chicken)

3 tablespoons crème fraîche

2 carrots, chopped (or you can use leftovers if you have them)

1 onion, peeled and chopped

1 tablespoon olive oil

1/2 teaspoon dried mixed herbs

1 litre (1 1/2 pints) vegetable stock (broth)

**SERVES
4**

188
calories
per serving

Method

Heat the oil in a saucepan, add the onion, carrots and mixed herbs and cook for 4 minutes. Add in the stock (broth) and chicken and bring it to the boil. Reduce the heat and simmer for 4 minutes. Stir in the crème fraîche. Using a hand blender or food processor blitz HALF of the soup until smooth, then return it to the saucepan, making sure it is warmed through before serving.

Mexican Chunky Soup

Ingredients

400g (14oz) tin cannellini beans, drained and rinsed

200g (7oz) chorizo sausage, sliced

3 large carrots, peeled and diced

1 onion, peeled and finely chopped

1 clove of garlic, crushed

1 teaspoon chilli powder

1 red pepper (bell pepper), deseeded and chopped

1 green pepper (bell pepper), deseeded and chopped

600mls (1 pint) warm vegetable stock (broth)

1 tablespoon olive oil

Salt

Freshly ground black pepper

SERVES 4

355 calories per serving

Method

Heat the oil in a large saucepan, add the chorizo and cook for 3 minutes. Remove it and set aside. Add in the onion, garlic and carrots. Cover and cook gently for about 5 minutes, stirring occasionally. Add in the chilli powder and vegetable stock (broth) and bring to the boil. Return the chorizo to the soup and add in the peppers (bell peppers) and cannellini beans. Season with salt and pepper. Serve into bowls.

Stilton & Celery Soup

SERVES 4

181
calories
per serving

Ingredients

450g (1lb) celery, chopped

150g (5oz) crème fraîche

75g (3oz) Stilton cheese

25g (1oz) butter

1 onion, peeled and chopped

600mls (1 pint) hot vegetable stock (broth)

Method

Heat the butter in a saucepan, add the onion and celery and cook for 1 minute. Pour in the stock (broth), bring to the boil then reduce the heat and simmer for around 8 minutes. Add in the crème fraîche and stir in the cheese until it has melted. Serve and eat straight away.

Carrot & Ginger Soup

Ingredients

750g (1lb 11oz) carrots, chopped

5cm (2 inch) chunk of fresh ginger, peeled and chopped

2 teaspoons turmeric

2 cloves of garlic, chopped

2 sticks celery, chopped

1 bay leaf

1 onion, peeled and chopped

1200mls (2 pints) vegetable stock (broth)

FOR THE GARNISH

A small handful coriander leaves, chopped

4 spring onions, sliced

1 green chilli, diced

2 teaspoons sesame oil

2 teaspoons lime juice

2 tablespoons olive oil

SERVES 4

178 calories per serving

Method

Heat the olive oil in a large saucepan. Add the onion, garlic, celery, carrots, bay leaf and cook for 10 minutes. Add in the ginger and turmeric. Mix well and cook for five minutes. Pour in the vegetable stock (broth). Bring it to the boil, reduce the heat and simmer for 15-20 minutes or until the carrots are tender. Remove the bay leaf. Using a food processor or hand blender, blitz the soup until smooth. Return it to the heat. In a bowl, mix together the coriander, spring onions (scallions), chilli, sesame oil, lime juice and olive oil. Serve the soup into bowls and spoon the coriander mixture onto each one. Eat straight away.

Bean, Vegetable & Parmesan Soup

Ingredients

200g (7oz) cannellini beans, drained

6 spring onions (scallions), chopped

2 tomatoes, de-seeded and chopped

2 small carrots, peeled and finely diced

2 cloves of garlic, crushed

1 small courgette (zucchini) finely diced

1 teaspoon dried mixed herbs

2 tablespoons Parmesan cheese, grated (shredded)

2 tablespoons tomato purée (paste)

600mls (1 pint) vegetable stock (broth)

1 teaspoon olive oil

SERVES 2

227 calories per serving

Method

Heat the olive oil in a saucepan, add the carrots, spring onions (scallions), courgette (zucchini) and garlic. Cook for 4 minutes, or until the vegetables have softened. Pour in the stock (broth), mixed herbs and the tomato purée (paste). Bring to the boil, reduce the heat and simmer for 10 minutes. Add the beans and tomatoes and warm them completely. Serve the soup with the Parmesan cheese sprinkled on top. Eat straight away.

Ham & Lentil Soup

Ingredients

100g (3½ oz) lentils

24 large florets of cauliflower, chopped

4 slices of ham, chopped

2 stalks of celery, chopped

2 cloves of garlic, chopped

2 carrots, peeled and chopped

1 tablespoon fresh parsley, chopped

1 onion, peeled and chopped

1 bay leaf

250mls (8fl oz) vegetable stock (broth)

Sea salt

Freshly ground black pepper

SERVES 2

169 calories per serving

Method

Place all of the ingredients into a saucepan. Bring it to the boil then reduce the heat and simmer for 30 minutes. Remove the bay leaf from the soup. Using a hand blender or food processor, blitz the soup until smooth. Season with salt and pepper then serve.

Cream of Chicken Soup

Ingredients

25g (1oz) butter

4 leeks, white part only, finely chopped

1 stick of celery, chopped

1 clove of garlic, chopped

1 chicken breast, cooked and finely chopped

600mls (1 pint) chicken stock (broth)

300mls (1/2 pint) whole milk

75mls (3fl oz) double cream

1 egg yolk

A large sprig of tarragon

Pinch of nutmeg

Sea salt

White pepper

SERVES 4

263
calories
per serving

Method

Heat the butter in a large saucepan. Add the celery, leeks, garlic and gently cook for 5 minutes. Pour in the chicken stock (broth) and the milk. Add the sprig of tarragon and simmer for 15 minutes. Remove the tarragon from the soup. Using a food processor or hand blender, process the soup until smooth. Add the cooked chicken to the blender and blitz until smooth. Return the soup to the heat and add the nutmeg. Season with salt and pepper. In a bowl, whisk together the double cream with the egg yolk. When the soup is really hot, remove it from the heat and gradually add the cream mixture whisking constantly until it has combined. Serve straight away.

Cream of Red Pepper Soup

Ingredients

2 red peppers (bell peppers), de-seeded and finely chopped

4 teaspoons half-fat crème fraîche

600mls (1 pint) hot stock (broth)

Sea salt

Freshly ground black pepper

SERVES 2

54 calories per serving

Method

Place the red peppers (bell peppers) into a saucepan and pour in the hot stock (broth). Bring it to the boil, reduce the heat and simmer for around 10 minutes until the peppers have softened. Using a hand blender or food processor, process until smooth. Stir in the crème fraîche and season with salt and pepper. Serve and enjoy.

Mediterranean Meatball Soup

Ingredients

2 x 400g (2 x 14oz) tinned chopped tomatoes

150g (5oz) baby spinach

100g (3½ oz) giant couscous

12 pork meatballs

2 red peppers (bell peppers), deseeded and chopped

1 onion, peeled and chopped

1 clove of garlic, chopped

½ teaspoon chilli flakes

600mls (1 pint) hot vegetable stock (broth)

1 tablespoon olive oil

A small bunch of fresh basil

SERVES 4

225 calories per serving

Method

Heat the oil in a large saucepan. Add the red peppers (bell peppers) and onion and cook for 6 minutes. Add in the chilli and garlic and stir well. Add in the vegetable stock (broth), couscous and tomatoes and bring it to the boil. Reduce the heat and allow it to simmer. Add in the meatballs and baby spinach and let it cook for 10 minutes or until the meatballs are cooked through. Serve the soup into bowls and add some basil on top. Eat straight away.

Lentil Bolognese Soup

Ingredients

500g (1lb 2oz) carton passata

125g (4oz) red lentils

125g (4oz) wholemeal pasta

50g (2oz) Parmesan cheese

4 cloves of garlic, finely chopped

4 sprigs fresh thyme

3 onions, finely chopped

3 large carrots, peeled and finely chopped

3 celery sticks, finely chopped

1 stock cube (bouillon cube)

1 teaspoon smoked paprika

2 litres hot water

2 tablespoons olive oil

SERVES 4

281 calories per serving

Method

Heat the oil in a large saucepan. Add in the onion and cook for 5 minutes. Add in the celery, carrots, garlic and cook for 5 minutes until the vegetables have softened. Pour in the passata, lentils, paprika, thyme and stock cube (bouillon cube). Pour in the hot water and season with salt and pepper. Allow it to simmer for 20 minutes. Add the pasta and lentils to the soup and cook for around 15 minutes or until they become tender. Stir occasionally. You can add a little extra water if you need to. Remove the sprigs of thyme and serve it into bowls.

Cauliflower & Walnut Soup

Ingredients

SERVES 4

165
calories
per serving

450g (1lb) cauliflower, chopped

12 walnuts halves, chopped

1 onion, peeled and chopped

600mls (1 pint) hot water

125mls (4fl oz) whole milk (or milk almond)

1 tablespoon olive oil

Method

Heat the oil in a saucepan, add the cauliflower and onion and cook for 2 minutes, stirring continuously. Pour in the hot water, bring to the boil and cook for 10 minutes. Stir in the milk. Using a food processor or hand blender, blitz the soup until smooth and creamy. Serve into bowls and add a sprinkle of walnuts.

Celeriac & Pear Soup

SERVES 4

153 calories per serving

Ingredients

2.5cm (1 inch) fresh root ginger

2 pears, cored, peeled and chopped

1 head of celeriac, peeled and chopped

1 onion, peeled and chopped

900mls (1½ pints) vegetable stock (broth)

2 tablespoons olive oil

Freshly ground black pepper

Method

Heat the oil in a saucepan, add the onion, celeriac, ginger and cook for 5 minutes. Pour in the vegetable stock (broth) and add the pear. Bring it to the boil, reduce the heat and simmer for 20-25 minutes. Using a hand blender or food processor, blend the soup until it's smooth. You can add extra stock (broth) or hot water to make the soup thinner if you wish. Season with pepper then serve.

Fennel & Butterbean Soup

Ingredients

400g (14oz) butter beans

2 large fennel bulbs, chopped

1 carrot, peeled and chopped

1 onion, peeled and chopped

1 courgette (zucchini), chopped

1 clove of garlic, chopped

900mls (1½ pints) vegetable stock (broth)

Sea salt

Freshly ground black pepper

SERVES 4

127 calories per serving

Method

Heat the vegetable stock (broth) in a large saucepan. Add in all of the vegetables but not the butterbeans just yet. Bring them to the boil, reduce the heat and simmer for 20 minutes. Add the butterbeans and stir until warmed through. Using a hand blender or food processor, process the soup until smooth. Season and serve.

Quick Lentil Soup

Ingredients

400g (14oz) tin of chopped tomatoes

350g (12oz) tinned green lentils (drained)

1 onion, peeled and chopped

1 teaspoon ground cumin

1 tablespoon olive oil

900mls (1½ pints) hot vegetable stock (broth)

SERVES 4

168 calories per serving

Method

Heat the oil in a frying pan, add the onion and cook for 4 minutes. Add in the vegetable stock (broth), tomatoes, lentils and cumin and bring it to a simmer for around 5 minutes. Use a hand blender or food processor and blitz until smooth. Serve and enjoy.

Broccoli & Cheddar Soup

Ingredients

175g (6oz) Cheddar cheese, grated (shredded)

1 head of broccoli, chopped

1 leek, chopped

1 courgette (zucchini), chopped

900mls (1½ pints) chicken stock (broth)

150mls (5fl oz) single cream

Sea salt

Freshly ground black pepper

SERVES 4

309 calories per serving

Method

Place the broccoli, leek and courgette (zucchini) in a saucepan and pour in the stock (broth). Bring them to the boil, reduce the heat and simmer for 15 minutes or until the vegetables are tender. Stir in the cream then using a hand blender or food processor blend until the soup becomes smooth. Add a little hot water or stock (broth) if you want to adjust the consistency. Season with salt and pepper. Sprinkle in the cheese and stir well. You can hold back a little and garnish with cheese when serving.

Chicken & Mushroom Soup

Ingredients

100g (3½ oz) cooked chicken, chopped

4 large mushrooms, finely sliced

6 spring onions (scallions), finely chopped

2 sticks of celery, finely chopped

2 teaspoons olive oil

600mls (1 pint) chicken stock (broth)

Sea salt

Freshly ground black pepper

SERVES 2

144 calories per serving

Method

Heat the oil in a saucepan, add the mushrooms, spring onions (scallions), celery and cook for 3-4 minutes. Pour in the stock (broth) and chopped chicken. Bring it to the boil, reduce the heat and cook for 10 minutes. Season with salt and pepper.

Quick Carrot & Coriander Soup

SERVES 4

91 calories per serving

Ingredients

5 medium carrots, peeled and chopped

1 onion, peeled and chopped

1 teaspoon ground coriander (cilantro)

1 tablespoon of olive oil

A large handful of fresh coriander (cilantro)

Sea salt

Freshly ground black pepper

900mls (1½ pints) vegetable stock (broth)

Fresh coriander (cilantro) for garnish

Method

Heat the oil in a saucepan, add the carrots and onion and cook for around 5 minutes until they have softened. Add in the stock (broth), ground and fresh coriander (cilantro) and bring it to the boil. Continue cooking for 10 minutes. Using a hand blender or food processor, blitz the soup until smooth and creamy. Season with salt and pepper. Serve into bowls and garnish with a little fresh coriander.

Smokey Squash & Tomato Soup

Ingredients

750g (1½ lb) butternut squash, peeled and diced

75g (3oz) baby spinach

6 tomatoes, quartered

4 cloves of garlic, chopped

2 red peppers (bell peppers), roughly chopped

1 teaspoon smoked paprika

1 teaspoon ground coriander

1 teaspoon ground cumin

900mls (1½ pints) vegetable stock (broth)

1 tablespoon tomato purée

TO SERVE

4 tablespoons natural (unflavoured) yogurt

A handful of fresh coriander (cilantro), chopped

SERVES 4

194 calories per serving

Method

Preheat the oven to 180C/360F. Place the butternut squash, peppers, tomatoes and garlic into an ovenproof dish. Sprinkle over the paprika, coriander, cumin and olive oil. Cook the vegetables in the oven for 20 minutes or until the vegetables have softened. Place half of them into a large saucepan and mash the remaining vegetables until they are pulpy. Add them to the saucepan and add the stock (broth) and tomato purée. Stir in the spinach and allow it to wilt for 5 minutes. Serve into bowls and add a swirl of cream and a sprinkle of fresh coriander (cilantro). Enjoy.

Miso Broth

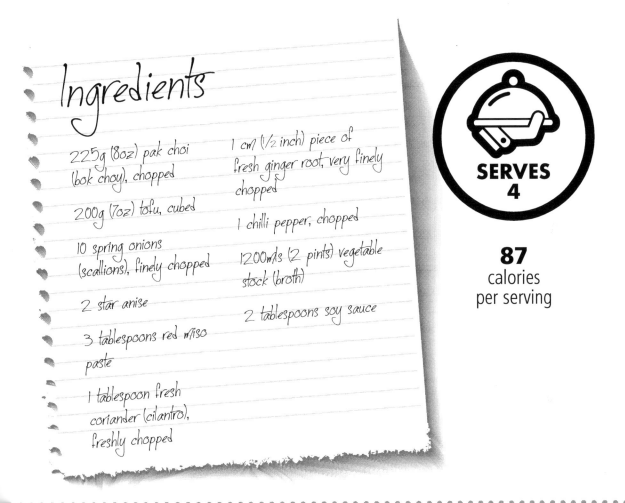

Ingredients

225g (8oz) pak choi (bok choy), chopped

200g (7oz) tofu, cubed

10 spring onions (scallions), finely chopped

2 star anise

3 tablespoons red miso paste

1 tablespoon fresh coriander (cilantro), freshly chopped

1 cm (½ inch) piece of fresh ginger root, very finely chopped

1 chilli pepper, chopped

1200mls (2 pints) vegetable stock (broth)

2 tablespoons soy sauce

SERVES 4

87 calories per serving

Method

Place the pak choi (bok choy) into a saucepan with the ginger, star anise, coriander, chilli and vegetable stock (broth). Bring to the boil, reduce the heat and simmer for 10 minutes. Add the spring onions (scallions), soy sauce and tofu. Cook for 3-4 minutes. In a bowl, mix together the red miso with a few tablespoons of the soup then stir the miso into the soup. Make sure the soup is warmed through. Serve into bowls.

Asparagus & Ham Soup

Ingredients

450g (1lb) asparagus spears, chopped

100g (3½ oz) ham, chopped

3 cloves of garlic, chopped

1 onion, peeled and chopped

1 handful of spinach leaves

1 tablespoon olive oil

750mls (1¼ pints) vegetable stock (broth)

Sea salt

Freshly ground black pepper

**SERVES
4**

113
calories
per serving

Method

Heat the oil in a saucepan, add the onion, garlic and asparagus and cook for 4 minutes. Add in the spinach and vegetable stock (broth) and cook for 5 minutes. Using a hand blender or food processor blitz the soup until smooth. Stir in the chopped ham. Season with salt and pepper and serve into bowls.

Gazpacho

Ingredients

10 tomatoes, de-seeded and chopped

5 cloves of garlic, chopped

2 red peppers (bell peppers), de-seeded and chopped

2 medium cucumbers, peeled and chopped

1 teaspoon chilli flakes

4 tablespoons apple cider vinegar

4 teaspoons olive oil

Sea salt

Freshly ground black pepper

**SERVES
4**

148
calories
per serving

Method

Place all of the ingredients into a food processor or blender and blitz until smooth. If the soup is too thick, just add a little extra oil or vinegar. Season with salt and pepper. Eat straight away or chill in the fridge before serving.

Courgette & Mint Soup

SERVES 4

235 calories per serving

Ingredients

6 courgettes (zucchinis), halved lengthways and thinly

3 cloves of garlic, chopped

1 onion, peeled and finely chopped

900mls (1½ pints) vegetable stock (broth)

150mls (5 fl oz) crème fraîche

2 tablespoons olive oil

A handful of fresh mint leaves, chopped

Zest of 1 lemon zest

Method

Heat the olive oil in a saucepan, add the onion and garlic cook for 5 minutes. Add the courgettes (zucchinis) and cook slowly for 20 minutes. Pour in the vegetable stock (broth), bring it to the boil and cook for around 5 minutes. Using a food processor or hand blender, process the soup until smooth. Stir in the crème fraîche and most of the mint – keep a little of the mint for garnish. Serve into bowls and sprinkle with a little mint.

Butternut Squash Soup With Goats Cheese Croutons

Ingredients

1kg (2lb) butternut squash, peeled and cubed

75g (3oz) soft goats cheese

4 slices sourdough, toasted

2 teaspoons cumin seeds

1 onion, peeled and finely chopped

1 red chilli, finely chopped

600mls (1 pint) vegetable (broth)

3 tablespoons olive oil

Sea salt

Freshly ground black pepper

SERVES 4

390 calories per serving

Method

Preheat the oven to 200C/400F. Scatter the squash on an ovenproof dish and coat it with a tablespoon of olive oil. Roast it in the oven for around 20 minutes or until tender. Remove it and set aside.Heat the oil in a frying pan, add the onion and cook for 5 minutes. Add the roasted squash, cumin and chilli to the saucepan and cook for 2 minutes before adding in the vegetable stock (broth). Bring it to the boil, reduce the heat and simmer for 10 minutes. Using a food processor or hand blender, blitz the soup until smooth. Season with salt and pepper. Spread the toasted sourdough with the goat's cheese. Serve the soup into bowls and serve with the toast. Enjoy straight away.

Spicy Tomato & Basil Soup

SERVES 2

97 calories per serving

Ingredients

2 x 400g (14oz) tin of chopped tomatoes

2 teaspoons tomato purée (paste)

½ courgette (zucchini), chopped

400mls (14fl oz) hot vegetable stock (broth)

Pinch of chilli flakes (or to taste)

Freshly ground black pepper

A handful of fresh basil leaves, chopped

Method

Place the tomatoes, purée, courgette, chilli, stock (broth) and half of the basil into a sauce-pan. Bring it to the boil, reduce the heat and simmer for 20 minutes, stirring occasionally. You can add some hot water if the soup seems too thick. Season with black pepper. Using a stick blender or food processor blitz the soup until smooth. Serve with a sprinkling of fresh basil. Enjoy.

Quick Thai Crab Soup

Ingredients

100g (3½ oz) cooked crab meat

1 teaspoon thai red curry paste

1 teaspoon fresh coriander (cilantro), chopped

½ green pepper (bell pepper), chopped

75mls (3fl oz) coconut milk

150mls (5fl oz) vegetable stock (broth)

1 teaspoon fish sauce

1 teaspoon olive oil

SERVES 1

303 calories per serving

Method

Heat the olive oil in a frying pan, add the green pepper (bell pepper) and cook for 4 minutes. Stir in the curry paste and pour in the stock (broth) and cook for 1 minute. Add in the fish sauce, crab meat and coconut milk and cook for around 10 minutes. Stir in the coriander (cilantro) and make sure the soup is warmed through.

Winter Spiced Pumpkin Soup

Ingredients

1kg (2¼lb) pumpkin

25g (1oz) butter

1 onion, chopped

¼ teaspoon nutmeg

½ teaspoon cinnamon

600mls (1 pint) vegetable stock (broth)

Sea salt

Freshly ground black pepper

SERVES 8

68 calories per serving

Method

Cut open the pumpkin, remove the seeds and discard. Cut the flesh into cubes. Heat the butter in a pan and add the onion. Cook it until it becomes soft. Add to the pan the pumpkin and the vegetable stock (broth). Bring it to the boil, reduce the heat and simmer for 30 minutes. Using a food processor or hand blender, process until smooth and creamy. Return to the pan and add the nutmeg, cinnamon, salt and pepper.

Prawn & Coconut Soup

Ingredients

450g (1lb) prawns (shrimp), peeled and de-veined

4 cloves of garlic, crushed

4cm (2 inch) chunk of fresh ginger, peeled and chopped

4 teaspoons lemongrass paste or 2 inner stalks, very finely chopped

1 teaspoon curry powder

1 lime, quartered for garnish

1 tablespoon fresh coriander (cilantro)

1/2 teaspoon chilli flakes

400mls (14fl oz) vegetable stock (broth)

600mls (1 pint) coconut milk

2 tablespoons olive oil

Sea salt

Freshly ground black pepper

SERVES 4

408 calories per serving

Method

Heat the olive oil in a large saucepan and add the ginger, garlic, lemongrass, curry powder and chilli flakes. Cook for around 1 minute. Pour in the stock (broth) and mix well. Bring it to the boil, reduce the heat and simmer gently. Add the prawns and cook for 3 minutes. Pour in the coconut milk and warm it through. Season with salt and pepper. Serve in bowls with a wedge of lime and sprinkling of coriander (cilantro).

Crab & Sweetcorn Soup

Ingredients

450g (1lb) sweetcorn

225g (8oz) crabmeat

4 spring onions (scallions), chopped

2 teaspoons cornflour (cornstarch)

2 tablespoons fresh coriander (cilantro) chopped

1cm (½inch) chunk fresh ginger, chopped

1 egg white

1200mls (2 pints) chicken stock (broth)

3 tablespoons soy sauce

SERVES 4

194 calories per serving

Method

Place the stock (broth), crab meat and sweetcorn into a wok or saucepan, bring to the boil and simmer for 15 minutes. Stir in the ginger, spring onions (scallions) and soy sauce. Simmer for 5 minutes. In a small bowl or cup, mix the cornflour (cornstarch) with a tablespoon or two of cold water. Pour the mixture into the soup and stir until the soup thickens slightly. In a bowl, whisk the egg white then pour it into the soup while constantly stirring. Sprinkle in the coriander (cilantro). Serve into bowls.

Slow Cooked Chicken Broth

Ingredients

450g (1lb) chicken breasts, chopped

400g (14oz) tinned tomatoes

75g (3oz) cabbage, finely chopped

4 celery stalks, chopped

3 cloves of garlic, chopped

1 onion, peeled and chopped

1 carrot, peeled and diced

1 leek, finely chopped

2 teaspoons dried mixed herbs

1 teaspoon dried coriander (cilantro)

2 tablespoons tomato purée (paste)

1 handful of fresh parsley, chopped

1200mls (2 pints) chicken stock (broth)

300mls (½ pint) hot water

Sea salt

Freshly ground black pepper

SERVES 4

246
calories
per serving

Method

Place all of the ingredients into a slow cooker and mix them well. Cook on high for 4-6 hours. If you prefer your soup thinner you can add a little extra hot water. Season with salt and pepper. Serve and enjoy.

Pistou Soup

SERVES 4

203
calories
per serving

Ingredients

400g (14oz) haricot beans, drained

200g (7oz) green beans, chopped

50g (2oz) Parmesan cheese, grated (shredded)

3 tomatoes, chopped

3 cloves of garlic, chopped

2 leeks, finely sliced

1 large courgette (zucchini), finely diced

1 litre (1½ pints) vegetable stock (broth)

1 tablespoon olive oil

A small handful of fresh basil

Sea salt

Freshly ground black pepper

Method

Heat the oil in a large saucepan. Add the courgette (zucchini) and leeks and cook for 5 minutes. Pour in the stock (broth), green beans, three-quarters of the haricot bean and half of the tomatoes and simmer for 8 minutes. In the meantime, put the remaining tomatoes, beans, basil and garlic into a food processor and blitz until smooth. Stir in the Parmesan to the processed mixture. Stir the sauce into the soup and cook for 2 minutes. Season with salt and pepper. Serve into bowls and enjoy.

Artichoke Soup

Ingredients

450g (1lb) Jerusalem artichokes, peeled and chopped

25g (1oz) butter

2 tablespoons grated (shredded) Parmesan cheese

1 onion, peeled and chopped

1 large potato, peeled and chopped

600mls (1 pint) vegetable stock (broth)

3 tablespoons double cream (heavy cream)

2 teaspoons olive oil

1 whole sprig of rosemary

Chopped leaves of 1 sprig of rosemary for garnish

Sea salt

Freshly ground black pepper

SERVES 4

447 calories per serving

Method

Heat the butter in a large saucepan. Add the onion, potato, and the whole sprig of rosemary and cook for 5 minutes. Add in the artichokes, cover with a lid and cook for 5 minutes, stirring occasionally. Pour in the stock (broth) and cook for 15 minutes until the vegetables are tender. Remove the sprig of rosemary. Using a food processor or hand blender, blitz the soup until smooth. Gently warm the soup and pour in the cream and season with salt and pepper. Serve into bowls with a sprinkling of Parmesan cheese and a little rosemary.

Red Pepper & Chickpea Soup

Ingredients

200g (6oz) tinned chickpeas (garbanzo beans), drained

3 red peppers (bell pepper), de-seeded and chopped

2 teaspoons ground coriander (cilantro)

1 onion, peeled and chopped

1 handful of fresh parsley, chopped

1200mls (2 pints) vegetable stock (broth)

1 tablespoon olive oil

Sea salt

Freshly ground black pepper

**SERVES
4**

150
calories
per serving

Method

Heat the oil in a large saucepan, add the onion and cook for 2 minutes. Add in the red peppers (bell pepper), ground coriander (cilantro) and stock (broth). Bring it to the boil, reduce the heat and simmer until the vegetables have softened. Using a hand blender or food processor and blitz until smooth. Return it to the saucepan, add the parsley and chickpeas (garbanzo beans) and warm them. Season with salt and pepper and serve.

Minestrone Soup

Ingredients

- 400g (14oz) tin of cannellini beans, drained
- 400g (14oz) tin of chopped tomatoes
- 100g (3½ oz) cabbage, shredded
- 100g (3½ oz) dried spaghetti, snapped into pieces
- 2 stalks of celery, chopped
- 2 medium courgettes (zucchinis), chopped
- 2 cloves of garlic, chopped
- 2 carrots, peeled and finely chopped
- 1 medium potato, peeled and diced
- 1 large onion, peeled and chopped
- 1 tablespoons tomato purée (tomato paste)
- 1 small bunch of basil leaves, shredded
- 900mls (1½ pints) vegetable stock (broth)
- 2 tablespoons olive oil
- A small handful of fresh parsley, chopped
- Sea salt
- Freshly ground black pepper

**SERVES
4**

355
calories
per serving

Method

Heat the oil in a large saucepan, add the onion, carrots, celery and garlic and cook for
10 minutes, stirring occasionally. Add in the stock (broth), tomatoes and tomato purée (paste),
bring to the boil, reduce the heat and simmer for 10 minutes. Add the potato, beans,
courgettes, cabbage and spaghetti and continue cooking for around 15 minutes or until the
vegetables have softened. Season with salt and pepper. Serve with a sprinkling of fresh parsley.

Carrot & Tomato Soup

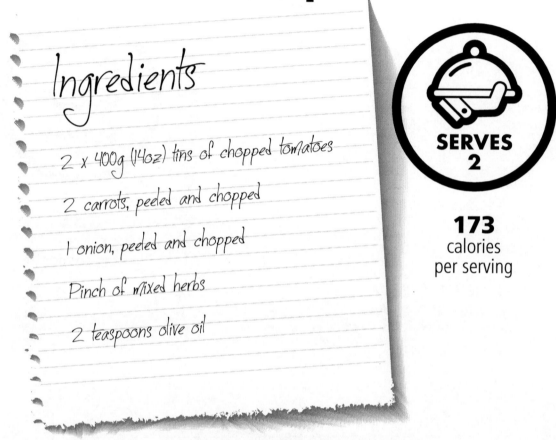

Ingredients

2 x 400g (14oz) tins of chopped tomatoes

2 carrots, peeled and chopped

1 onion, peeled and chopped

Pinch of mixed herbs

2 teaspoons olive oil

SERVES 2

173 calories per serving

Method

Heat the oil in a saucepan, add the onion and cook for 3 minutes. Add in the carrot and cook for 2 minutes. Stir in the chopped tomatoes and add around a cup of warm water or enough to cover the ingredients. Simmer gently for around 15 minutes or until the carrots have softened, stirring occasionally. Add some extra hot water if required. Stir in the mixed herbs. Use a stick blender or cool the soup slightly and place it in a food processor until smooth. Serve and enjoy.

Cream of Celery Soup

**SERVES
2**

163
calories
per serving

Ingredients

8 stalks of celery, chopped

2 cloves of garlic, chopped

1 onion, peeled and chopped

600mls (1 pint) vegetable stock (broth)

2 tablespoons crème fraîche

1 tablespoon olive oil

A small handful of fresh parsley

Method

Heat the olive oil in a saucepan, add the onion, celery and garlic and cook for 5 minutes until the vegetables have softened. Add in the stock (broth), bring it to the boil, reduce the heat and simmer for around 15 minutes. Stir in the crème fraîche. Using a food processor or hand blender process the soup until smooth and creamy. Serve with a sprinkling of parsley.

Avocado, Lime & Coriander (Cilantro) Soup

Ingredients

1 large avocado, peeled and de-stoned

6 tablespoons crème fraîche

2 tablespoons of coriander (cilantro), chopped

900mls (1½ pints) vegetable stock (broth)

Juice from ½ lime

Sea salt

Freshly ground black pepper

SERVES 4

168 calories per serving

Method

Place the avocado and half the crème fraîche into a blender and blitz until smooth. In a saucepan, heat the vegetable stock (broth) and add the remaining crème fraîche. Squeeze the lime juice into the avocado mixture and stir well. Gradually stir the avocado mixture into the warm vegetable stock, keeping it on a low heat until it is completely combined. Add in the coriander (cilantro) and season with salt and pepper. Serve into bowls. Eat straight away.

Turkey & Vegetable Broth

Ingredients

450g (1lb) fresh turkey breast steaks, chopped

400g (14oz) tin of chopped tomatoes

200g (7oz) brown lentils, rinsed

100g (3½ oz) pearl barley

75g (3oz) cabbage, finely chopped

3 stalks of celery, finely chopped

2 cloves of garlic, chopped

1 carrot, peeled and diced

1 onion, peeled and chopped

1 handful of fresh spinach leaves

1 teaspoon dried mixed herbs

2 tablespoons tomato purée (paste)

1 small handful of fresh parsley, chopped

1200mls (2 pints) chicken stock (broth)

300mls (½ pint) hot water

Sea salt

Freshly ground black pepper

**SERVES
6**

208
calories
per serving

Method

Place all of the ingredients, except the parsley, salt and pepper, into a slow cooker and stir well. Cook on high for around 6 hours. If you prefer your soup thinner you can add a little extra hot water. Sprinkle in the parsley and stir well. Season with salt and pepper. Serve into bowls.

Roast Sausage & Bean Soup

Ingredients

- 125g (4oz) chorizo sausage, chopped
- 200g (7oz) tinned chickpeas (garbanzo beans)
- 200g (7oz) tinned haricot beans
- 1 red pepper (bell pepper), deseeded and chopped
- 4 ripe medium tomatoes, roughly chopped
- 3 cloves of garlic, chopped
- 2 teaspoons paprika
- 1 tablespoon tomato purée
- 1 onion, peeled and chopped
- 900mls (1½ pints) vegetable stock (broth)
- 2 tablespoons olive oil
- 2 teaspoons balsamic vinegar
- Sea salt
- Freshly ground black pepper
- A handful of fresh basil, chopped

SERVES 4

349 calories per serving

Method

Spread the chorizo, tomatoes, onions, garlic and red pepper onto an ovenproof dish and drizzle the ingredients with olive oil. Roast them in the oven for 15 minutes. Put half these roasted ingredients to one side. Use a food processor or hand blender to blend the other half of the roasted ingredients until smooth. Place all of the ingredients, except the basil, into a large saucepan. Bring it to the boil, reduce the heat and simmer for 15 minutes. Season with salt and pepper. Serve with a sprinkle of fresh basil on top.

Butternut Squash & Orange Soup

Ingredients

SERVES 4

134 calories per serving

1 butternut squash, peeled, de-seeded and chopped

1 onion, peeled and chopped

1 teaspoon ground coriander (cilantro)

1 tablespoon olive oil

1200mls (2 pints) hot water

Grated zest and juice of 1 orange

A small handful of fresh coriander (cilantro)

Method

Heat the oil in a saucepan, add the onion and cook for 5 minutes. Add in the squash and cook for 5 minutes. Stir in the ground coriander (cilantro), orange zest and hot water. Reduce the heat and simmer for 10 minutes. Stir in the coriander (cilantro) and orange juice. Using a hand blender or food processor blend the soup until smooth. Re-heat if necessary before serving. Serve with a sprinkling of coriander.

Sweetcorn & Bacon Chowder

SERVES 2

418 calories per serving

Ingredients

200g (7oz) sweetcorn

3 rashers of streaky bacon, chopped

1 onion, peeled and finely chopped

1 potato, peeled and cubed

350mls (12 fl oz) vegetable stock (broth)

350mls (12fl oz) whole milk

1 tablespoon olive oil

A small handful of fresh chives, chopped

Method

Heat the oil in a frying pan and add in the bacon. Cook it for around 3 minutes then add the potato and onion. Cook until they begin to soften. Add in the vegetable stock (broth) and milk and allow it to simmer for around 10 minutes or until the potato is completely cooked. Add in the sweetcorn and warm it through. Serve into bowls with a sprinkle of chives.

Root Vegetable Soup

SERVES 4

125 calories per serving

Ingredients

3 courgette (zucchinis), chopped

3 carrots, peeled and chopped

1 onion, peeled and chopped

1 sweet potato, peeled and chopped

1 teaspoon dried mixed herbs

1 small handful of fresh parsley

1 small handful of fresh thyme

600mls (1 pint) stock (broth)

1 tablespoon olive oil

Sea salt

Freshly ground black pepper

Method

Heat the olive oil in a saucepan, add the vegetables and cook for 5 minutes or until they have started to soften. Add the stock (broth) and dried herbs and cook on a medium heat for 20-30 minutes or until the vegetables are cooked through. Stir in the fresh herbs. Use a hand blender or food processor and blitz until smooth. Season with salt and pepper and serve.

Bacon & Roast Sweet Potato Soup

SERVES 4

259 calories per serving

Ingredients

3 medium sweet potatoes, peeled and cut into chunks

4 rashers of bacon, chopped

2 teaspoons garlic powder

2 teaspoons paprika

1 onion, peeled and finely chopped

900mls (1½ pints) vegetable stock (broth)

2 tablespoons olive oil

Sea Salt

Freshly ground black pepper

Method

Pre-heat the oven to 200C/400F. Coat the sweet potato with a tablespoon of olive oil and roast it in the oven for around 20 minutes or until it is tender. Meanwhile, heat a tablespoon of oil in a saucepan and add the bacon. Cook it for around 5 minutes, stirring occasionally. Add the paprika, onion and garlic and cook for 5 minutes. Pour in the stock (broth) and simmer gently. Remove the sweet potato from the oven and add it to the soup mixture. Using a hand blender or food processor, blend only HALF of the soup, before returning it to the saucepan. Season with salt and pepper. Heat it gently then serve it into bowls with a little sprinkling of paprika to garnish.

Spiced Parsnip Soup

Ingredients

- 450g (1lb) parsnips, peeled and chopped
- 2 carrots, peeled and chopped
- 1 onion, peeled and chopped
- 1 stick of celery, chopped
- 1 teaspoon garam masala
- 1 teaspoon paprika
- 1/2 teaspoon chilli flakes
- 900mls (1½ pints) vegetable stock (broth)
- 4 tablespoons double cream (heavy cream)

to garnish
- 1 tablespoon of olive oil

**SERVES
4**

216
calories
per serving

Method

Heat the oil in a frying pan, add the onion and cook for 5 minutes. Add in the parsnip and carrot and cook until they have softened. Add in the garam masala, chilli flakes and paprika and vegetable stock (broth). Bring it to the boil and simmer for around 15 minutes. Using a hand blender or food processor blitz the soup until smooth. Season with salt and pepper. Serve with a swirl of cream.

Stilton & Watercress Soup

Ingredients

225g (8oz) watercress, tough or thick stalks removed

150g (5oz) Stilton cheese, crumbled

150mls (5fl oz) plain natural yogurt (unflavoured)

600mls (1pint) vegetable stock (broth)

SERVES 4

197 calories per serving

Method

Pour the vegetable stock (broth) into a large saucepan and bring to the boil. Gently simmer for around 3 minutes or until the watercress is tender. Scatter the cheese into the soup and simmer for 1-2 minutes or until the cheese has melted. Pour the soup into a blender and blitz until smooth. Pour the blended soup back into the saucepan. Stir in the yogurt and heat it gently. Serve and enjoy.

Broccoli & Pesto Soup

Ingredients

6 large broccoli florets

1 vegetable stock (bouillon) cube

2 teaspoons pesto sauce

4 teaspoons crème fraîche

600mls (1 pint) hot water

Sea salt

Freshly ground black pepper

SERVES 2

61 calories per serving

Method

Pour the water into a saucepan, add the broccoli and cook for around 8-10 minutes or until the broccoli is soft. Add in the stock (broth) cube and stir until it dissolves. Using a hand blender or food processor whizz the soup until smooth. Stir in the pesto sauce and crème fraîche. Season with salt and black pepper to taste and serve into bowls.

Cream of Pumpkin Soup

Ingredients

900g (2lb) fresh pumpkin, peeled and de-seeded

2 teaspoons butter

1 onion, peeled and chopped

1/4 teaspoon nutmeg

1/4 teaspoon ground ginger

1/4 teaspoon cinnamon

600mls (1 pint) vegetable stock (broth)

150mls (5fl oz) double cream (or crème fraîche)

Sea salt

Freshly ground black pepper

SERVES 6

166 calories per serving

Method

Cut the pumpkin into chunks and place it in the slow cooker. Add in the butter, onion, nutmeg, ginger, cinnamon and stock (broth). Stir well. Cook on low for 5-6 hours or on high for 3-4 hours. Using a hand blender or food processor, blitz the soup until smooth. Stir in the cream and season with salt and pepper. Serve and enjoy.

Tomato & Quinoa Soup

Ingredients

400g (14oz) tinned tomatoes

400g (14oz) butterbeans

175g (6oz) quinoa, rinsed well

1 onion, peeled and chopped

1 bay leaf

1 small handful of fresh parsley, chopped

3 cloves of garlic, crushed

½ teaspoon dried basil

½ teaspoon dried oregano

½ teaspoon dried thyme

750mls (1¼ pints) vegetable stock (broth)

Sea salt

Freshly ground black pepper

SERVES 4

171 calories per serving

Method

Place the tomatoes, quinoa, onion, butterbeans, garlic and herbs into a slow cooker. Pour in the vegetable stock (broth) and stir well. Season with salt and pepper. Cook on low for 7 hours or on high for 3 hours. Sprinkle in the parsley and remove the bay leaf before serving.

Tom Yum Soup

Ingredients

150g (5oz) raw peeled prawns (shrimps)

125g (4oz) button mushrooms, quartered

2.5cm (1 inch) chunk of fresh ginger root, thinly sliced

2 cloves of garlic, crushed

2 kaffir lime leaves, thinly sliced

2 medium tomatoes, roughly chopped

2 teaspoons soft light brown sugar

1 lemongrass, bruised

1 bird's-eye chilli, chopped

Juice of 1 lime

1 tablespoon fish sauce

750mls (1¼ pints) chicken stock (broth)

SERVES 2

114 calories per serving

Method

Heat the chicken stock (broth) in a large saucepan and bring it to the boil. Add in the ginger, lemongrass, chilli, garlic and torn kaffir lime leaves and simmer for 15 minutes. Add the mushrooms and tomatoes and simmer for 5 minutes. Add in the prawns and simmer for 4-5 minutes or until they become pink. Remove the lemongrass and lime leaves and discard them. Add the lime juice, sugar and fish sauce, and serve.

Beetroot & Horseradish Soup

Ingredients

450g (1lb) potatoes, peeled and chopped

650g (1½ lb) beetroot, peeled and chopped

4 tablespoons of hot horseradish sauce

1 onion, peeled and sliced

600mls (1 pint) hot water

600mls (1pint) vegetable stock (broth)

100mls (3½ fl oz) soured cream

A small handful of fresh dill

2 tablespoons olive oil

SERVES 6

184 calories per serving

Method

Heat a tablespoon of olive oil in a large saucepan. Add in the onion and cook for 5 minutes or until it has softened. Add in the beetroot and potatoes and cook for 4 minutes, stirring continuously. Pour in the vegetable stock (broth) and 600mls (1 pint) of hot water. Bring it to the boil, then simmer for 20 minutes or until the vegetables are tender. Add in half of the sourced cream and stir. Using a hand blender or food processor, blitz until smooth. Season with salt and pepper. Serve with a swirl of cream and a sprinkle of dill. Enjoy.

Sweet Potato Korma Soup

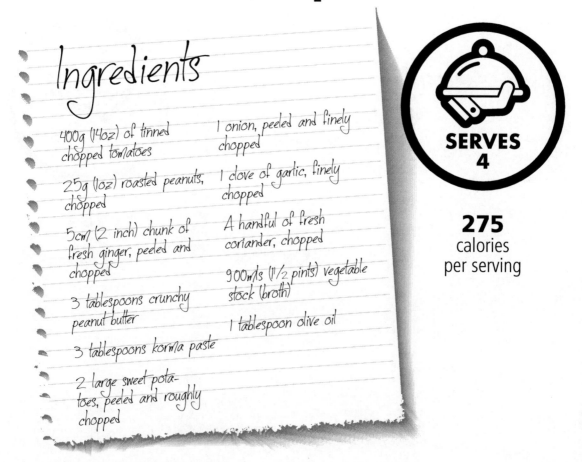

Ingredients

400g (14oz) of tinned chopped tomatoes

25g (1oz) roasted peanuts, chopped

5cm (2 inch) chunk of fresh ginger, peeled and chopped

3 tablespoons crunchy peanut butter

3 tablespoons korma paste

2 large sweet potatoes, peeled and roughly chopped

1 onion, peeled and finely chopped

1 clove of garlic, finely chopped

A handful of fresh coriander, chopped

900mls (1½ pints) vegetable stock (broth)

1 tablespoon olive oil

SERVES 4

275 calories per serving

Method

Heat the oil in a large saucepan, add the onion and cook for 5 minutes. Add in the ginger and coriander and cook for 1 minute. Add in the sweet potato and korma paste and cook for 1 minute. Pour in the stock (broth) and cook for 20 minutes or until the sweet potato is tender. Add in the peanut butter and stir well. Using a hand blender or food processor, blitz the soup until smooth. Serve into bowls with a sprinkling of coriander.

Chilli Bean Soup

SERVES 4

285
calories
per serving

Ingredients

- 2 x 400g (2 x 14oz) tins of chopped tomatoes
- 2 x 400g (2 x 14oz) tins of red kidney beans
- 50g (2oz) butter
- 2 sticks of celery, chopped
- 2 vegetable stock cubes (bouillon cubes)
- 1 red pepper (bell pepper), deseeded and chopped
- 1 onion, peeled and chopped
- 1 teaspoon chilli powder
- 2 teaspoons balsamic vinegar
- Salt and freshly ground black pepper

Method

Melt the butter in a saucepan and add the onion and celery and cook for 5 minutes or until they have softened. Add in the red pepper and cook for 2 minutes. Add in the tomatoes, chilli powder, kidney beans, stock cubes (bouillon cubes), balsamic vinegar and 180mls (6fl oz) of water. Bring it to the boil, reduce the heat and simmer for 15-20 minutes. Season with salt and pepper and serve.

Spanish Prawn Soup

Ingredients

400g (14oz) chopped tomatoes

200g (7oz) raw king prawns

3 cloves of garlic, crushed

1 carrot, peeled and finely chopped

1 celery stick, chopped

1 green chilli, chopped

1 tablespoon tomato purée

1 sweet potato, peeled and diced

1 avocado, stoned removed and chopped

1 red onion, chopped

1 smoked paprika

1 teaspoon ground cumin

1 teaspoon dried oregano

1 lime, wedged

1 tablespoon olive oil

A small bunch of coriander (cilantro), chopped

SERVES 4

160 calories per serving

Method

Heat the oil in a large saucepan, add the carrot, celery, chilli and onion and cook for 10 minutes. Add in the paprika, cumin, garlic, tomato puree and oregano, and cook for 2 minutes. Add in the tomatoes, sweet potato and 350mls (12 fl oz) of water. Bring it to the boil, reduce the heat and simmer for 30 minutes. Add the prawns and simmer for 5 minutes until they are cooked through and have turned pink. In a small bowl, mix together the avocado and coriander (cilantro). Serve the soup into bowls and spoon some avocado onto each one. Add a wedge of lime and eat straight away.

Pork & Noodle Soup

SERVES 4

234
calories
per serving

Ingredients

250g (9oz) pork fillet, finely sliced

150g (5oz) cooked rice

100g (3½ oz) rice noodles, snapped in half

2 cloves of garlic, finely chopped

2.5cm (1 inch) chunk of fresh ginger, peeled and chopped

2 small red chillies, de-seeded and finely chopped

1 whole star anise

1 shallot, finely chopped

600mls (1 pint) hot water

600mls (1 pint) chicken stock (broth)

1 tablespoon fish sauce

1 tablespoon groundnut oil

A handful of basil leaves, finely sliced

Sea salt

Freshly ground black pepper

Method

Heat the oil in a saucepan, add the garlic, shallot, star anise and ginger and stir for 1 minute. Add in the chicken stock (broth), hot water, chilli and bring them to the boil. Add the pork and noodles and simmer for 15 minutes until the noodles are soft and the pork is cooked. Stir in the rice and fish sauce and warm it through. Season with salt and pepper. Stir in the fresh basil and serve the soup into bowls.

Spiced Lamb & Chickpea Soup

Ingredients

400g (14oz) tinned chopped tomatoes

400g (14oz) cooked chickpeas (garbanzo beans), drained and rinsed

225g (8oz) lamb fillet, cut into thin strips

100g (3½ oz) baby spinach leaves

50g (2oz) feta cheese, crumbled

1 onion, peeled and chopped

1 clove of garlic, crushed

1 teaspoon harissa paste

600mls (1 pint) hot vegetable stock (broth)

1 tablespoon olive oil

Sea salt

Freshly ground black pepper

SERVES 4

299 calories per serving

Method

Heat the oil in a large saucepan, add the lamb and cook for 3 minutes, stirring constantly. Remove it and set it aside. Add the onion to the saucepan and cook for 5 minutes. Add the harissa paste and garlic and cook for 1 minute. Add in the tomatoes and stock (broth), bring it to the boil and simmer for five minutes. Add in the chickpeas (garbanzo beans) and cook for a further five minutes. Return the lamb to the saucepan and warm it through. Stir in the spinach and season with salt and pepper. Serve into bowls with some feta cheese on top.

Fish Soup

Ingredients

- 400g (14oz) tinned chopped tomatoes
- 300g (11oz) small pasta shells
- 250g (9oz) monkfish tail, bones removed and flesh cubed
- 250g (9oz) frozen mixed seafood, defrosted and rinsed
- 50g (2oz) pitted olives, chopped
- 8 tomatoes, chopped
- 4 cloves of garlic, finely chopped
- 2 anchovy fillets in oil, drained
- 2 onions, peeled and finely chopped
- 2 carrots, peeled and finely chopped
- 2 celery stalks, finely chopped
- 2 red peppers (bell peppers), finely chopped
- 1800mls (approx. 3 pints) vegetable stock (broth)
- 600mls (1 pint) fish stock
- Sea salt
- Freshly ground black pepper
- 1 tablespoon olive oil

**SERVES
6**

290
calories
per serving

Method

Heat the olive oil and add the carrots, onion, garlic, celery and peppers and cook for 5 minutes. Add in the chopped tomatoes, fish and vegetable stock, anchovy fillets and fresh tomatoes. Bring it to the boil, reduce the heat and simmer for around 40 minutes. Add in the monkfish, mixed seafood and pasta. Cover and simmer for 40 minutes, stirring occasionally. Season with salt and pepper. Serve into bowls and add the olives on top. It goes beautifully with fresh crusty bread.

Chicken & Sweetcorn Soup

SERVES 4

247 calories per serving

Ingredients

300g (11oz) tinned sweetcorn, drained

4 spring onions, sliced

2.5cm (1 inch) chunk of fresh ginger, peeled and chopped

2 cloves of garlic, chopped

2 cooked chicken breasts, shredded

2 eggs, beaten

1200mls (2 pints) chicken stock (broth)

1 tablespoon soy sauce

1 tablespoon olive oil

A large handful of fresh coriander (cilantro), chopped

Sea salt

Freshly ground black pepper

Method

Heat the oil in a large saucepan and add the ginger, garlic and spring onions (scallions) and cook until softened. In the meantime, using a food processor or hand blender, blitz the sweetcorn to a smooth paste and set it aside. Pour the chicken stock (broth) and soy sauce into the saucepan, bring it to the boil, reduce the heat and stir in the sweetcorn. Add in the chicken and warm it through. Remove the saucepan from the heat and pour in the beaten egg, stirring continuously creating little shreds of egg throughout the soup. Season with salt and pepper. Serve into bowls with a sprinkle of coriander (cilantro).

Sweet Potato, Lime & Chilli Soup

Ingredients

3 medium sweet potatoes, peeled and chopped

1 onion, peeled and chopped

1 clove of garlic, chopped

1200mls (2 pints) vegetable stock (broth)

1 tablespoon olive oil

Zest and juice of 1/2 lime

Pinch chilli flakes

SERVES 4

156
calories
per serving

Method

Heat the oil in a large saucepan. Add the garlic and onion and cook for 5 minutes. Add the sweet potatoes and chilli flakes and cook for 2 minutes. Pour in the vegetable stock (broth) and simmer for 15 minutes. Using a food processor or hand blender, blitz the soup until smooth. Serve into bowls and add the lime juice and zest.

Barley & Vegetable Soup

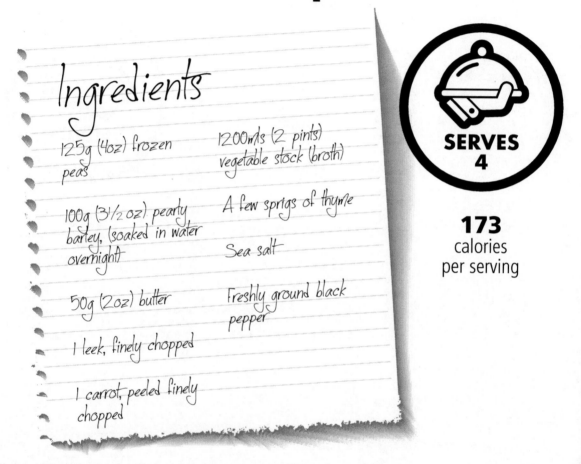

Ingredients

125g (4oz) frozen peas

100g (3½ oz) pearly barley, (soaked in water overnight

50g (2oz) butter

1 leek, finely chopped

1 carrot, peeled finely chopped

1200mls (2 pints) vegetable stock (broth)

A few sprigs of thyme

Sea salt

Freshly ground black pepper

SERVES 4

173 calories per serving

Method

Heat the butter in a large saucepan, add the leek and carrot and cook for around 7 minutes or until tender. Add the pearl barley and stir well, making sure it gets well coated in the butter. Add the stock (broth) and sprigs of thyme. Simmer for 25 minutes. Add in the peas and warm them through. Remove the thyme sprigs. Season with salt and pepper. Serve into bowls and garnish with a few thyme leaves.

Cannellini & Courgette Soup

Ingredients

400g (14oz) tinned cannellini beans in water, drained

2 courgette (zucchini), de-seeded and finely diced

1 clove of garlic, chopped

1 onion, finely chopped

½ leek, halved, finely sliced and soaked in water

900mls (1½ pints) vegetable stock (broth)

100mls (3fl oz) milk

2 tablespoons olive oil

A large handful of fresh parsley, chopped

SERVES 4

207 calories per serving

Method

Heat the olive oil in a large saucepan. Add the onions and cook for 5 minutes. Add the leek, courgette (zucchini), cannellini beans and cook for another 5 minutes. Pour in the stock and milk and simmer for 20 minutes. Season with salt and pepper. Stir in the parsley and serve into bowls. Enjoy.

Thai Style Squash Soup

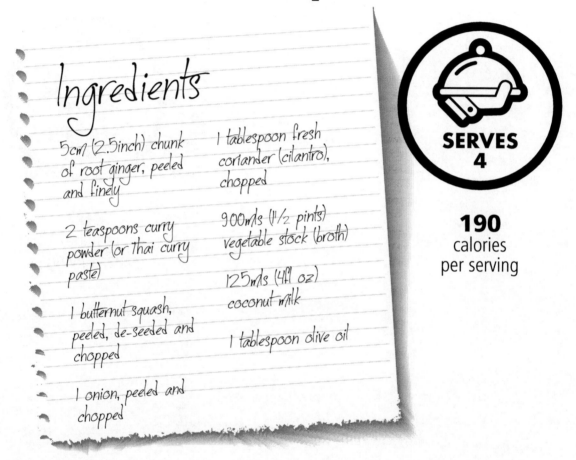

Ingredients

5cm (2.5inch) chunk of root ginger, peeled and finely

2 teaspoons curry powder (or thai curry paste)

1 butternut squash, peeled, de-seeded and chopped

1 onion, peeled and chopped

1 tablespoon fresh coriander (cilantro), chopped

900mls (1½ pints) vegetable stock (broth)

125mls (4fl oz) coconut milk

1 tablespoon olive oil

SERVES 4

190 calories per serving

Method

Heat the oil in a saucepan, add the onion and cook until it softens. Add the squash, curry powder (or paste), ginger and vegetable stock (broth). Bring the soup to the boil, reduce the heat and simmer for 20 minutes or until the squash is soft. Using a hand blender or a food processor, blitz the soup until smooth. It's advisable to let it cool slightly before transferring it to a food processor. Stir in the coconut milk and warm the soup completely. Serve into bowls with a sprinkling of coriander (cilantro).

Celeriac Soup With Herb Croutons

Ingredients

100g (3½ oz) Cheddar cheese

1 head of celeriac

1 onion, peeled and chopped

1 bay leaf

900mls (1½ pints) vegetable stock (broth)

50mls (2fl oz) double cream (heavy cream)

FOR THE CROUTONS:

2 slices of thick white bread

1 tablespoon of butter

Pinch of mixed herbs

SERVES 6

212 calories per serving

Method

Heat some olive oil in a saucepan, add the onion and cook for around 5 minutes or until it softens. Add in the vegetable stock (broth) and bay leaf and bring it to a simmer. Gently add in the celeriac and allow it to cook for around 15 minutes. Remove the bay leaf then using a food processor or hand blender, blitz the soup until smooth. Stir in the cream and add the cheese and stir well. In the meantime, butter the bread and sprinkle on the mixed herbs onto the butter. Remove the crusts and cut the bread into cubes. Heat a frying pan and add the bread cubes. Fry them until they are golden. Serve the soup into bowls and scatter some croutons on top.

Leek & Potato Soup

SERVES 4

330 calories per serving

Ingredients

200g (7oz) smoked salmon, thinly sliced

25g (1oz) butter

3 large floury potatoes, peeled and chopped

2 large leeks, trimmed, sliced and rinsed

1200mls (2 pints) vegetable stock (broth)

100mls (3½ fl oz) crème fraîche

A small handful of fresh chives, chopped

Sea salt

Freshly ground black pepper

Method

Heat the butter in a large saucepan. Add in the potatoes and the leeks and cook for 10 minutes until they have softened. Pour in the stock (broth). Bring it to the boil, reduce the heat and simmer for 30 minutes. Add in the crème fraîche and using a food processor or hand blender, process the soup until smooth. Season with salt and pepper. When you are ready to serve, add in most of the smoked salmon, keeping back a little for garnish. Serve it into bowls with a sprinkling of chives and a little of the smoked salmon. Enjoy straight away.

Asian Beef Noodle Soup

Ingredients

450g (1lb) beef, cut into chunks

300g (11oz) noodles

5cm (2 inch) chunk of fresh ginger

4 spring onions (scallions), chopped

2 carrots, peeled and chopped

2 cloves of garlic, peeled

2 tablespoon tomato purée

1 handful baby spinach leaves, shredded

1 red chilli, seeded and shredded

1 onion, peeled and sliced

1 star anise

1 tablespoon fish sauce

1 lime, cut into wedges

900mls (1½ pints) beef stock (broth)

A large handful of coriander (cilantro), chopped

A spring onion (scallion), chopped for garnish

SERVES 4

361 calories per serving

Method

Heat the beef stock (broth) in a large saucepan together with the onion, carrots, chilli, garlic, star anise, ginger, fish sauce and tomato purée. Bring it to the boil, then reduce the heat. Add in the beef and simmer for 40 minutes. Remove the garlic, ginger and star anise. Add the noodles and cook them in the soup for the length of time on the instruction packet. Serve the soup into bowls and scatter the spring onions (scallions), spinach and a lime wedge.

Cauliflower & Coconut Soup

Ingredients

25g (1oz) butter

1 onion, peeled and finely chopped

1 whole cauliflower, divided into florets

1 large potato, peeled and diced

1 clove of garlic, chopped

½ red chilli, deseeded and finely chopped (optional)

2 tablespoons fish sauce

600mls (1 pint) vegetable stock (broth)

400mls (14fl oz) light coconut milk

Sea salt

Freshly ground black pepper

1 lime, cut into wedges

SERVES 4

228 calories per serving

Method

Heat the butter in a saucepan, add the onion and cook for 5 minutes. Add the cauliflower, potato, chilli and garlic and cook until they have softened. Add the fish sauce and stock (broth). Bring it to the boil, reduce the heat and simmer for 20 minutes or until the cauliflower is completely cooked. Using a food processor or hand blender, blitz the soup until smooth. Stir in the coconut milk and warm it through. Serve into bowls and add a wedge of lime to squeeze over the top.

Beef Goulash Soup

Ingredients

450g (1lb) beef, cubed

400g (14oz) tinned chopped tomatoes

6 tablespoons sour cream

3 tablespoons paprika

3 garlic cloves, crushed

1 large onion, peeled and chopped

1 teaspoon caraway seeds

1 large potato, peeled and cubed

1 parsnip, peeled and chopped

1 carrot, peeled and chopped

1 celery stalk, chopped

1 green pepper (bell pepper), deseeded and chopped

A small handful of fresh parsley, chopped

600mls (1 pint) beef stock (broth)

2 tablespoon olive oil

SERVES 8

429 calories per serving

Method

Heat oil in large pan and fry the beef for 5 minutes until golden. Add the onion, garlic and caraway seeds and cook for 5 minutes. Add the beef stock (broth) and paprika and bring it to the boil. Add in the beef and cook for around 40 minutes. Add in the vegetables and tinned tomatoes. Reduce the heat and simmer for 20 minutes or until the vegetables are cooked through. Using a food processor or hand blender, blitz only HALF of the mixture until roughly chopped, then combine it back with the rest of the soup. You can add some extra hot stock or water if you need to thin the texture of the soup. Warm the soup completely then serve it into bowls with a dollop of sour cream and a sprinkling of parsley.

Cabbage, Bacon & Bean Soup

Ingredients

400g (14oz) tinned haricot beans, drained and rinsed

150g (5oz) bacon, chopped

2 carrots, peeled and finely diced

2 celery stalks, finely diced

2 cloves of garlic, crushed

1 onion, peeled and chopped

½ small savoy cabbage, shredded

1 tablespoon fresh thyme leaves

900mls (1½ pints) vegetable stock (broth)

1 tablespoon olive oil

Sea salt

Freshly ground black pepper

SERVES 4

311 calories per serving

Method

Heat the oil in a large saucepan, add the bacon and cook until it becomes golden. Remove it and set it aside. Add the onion, carrots, celery, thyme and garlic to the saucepan and cook for about 5 minutes. Return the bacon to the pan and add the beans and stock (broth). Bring it to the boil, reduce the heat and simmer for 15 minutes. Add in the cabbage and continue cooking for 7 minutes. Season with salt and pepper. Serve and enjoy.

Cucumber, Lettuce & Pea Soup

Ingredients

225g (8oz) frozen peas

8 spring onions, chopped

4 slices rye bread

1 cucumber, roughly chopped

1 lettuce, chopped

1500mls (3 pints) vegetable stock (broth)

1 teaspoon olive oil

SERVES 4

211 calories per serving

Method

Heat the oil in a large saucepan and add the spring onions. Cook for around 3 minutes, stirring occasionally. Add the peas, cucumber, lettuce and vegetable stock (broth) and simmer for 10 minutes. Using a hand blender or food processor, blitz the soup until smooth. Serve with a slice of rye bread. This soup can also be served cold.

You may also be interested in other titles by
Erin Rose Publishing
which are available in both paperback and ebook.

 **Quick Start Guides**

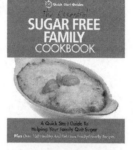

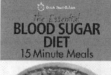
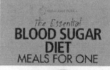

The Essential
HEALTHY GUT DIET
RECIPE BOOK

A Quick Start Guide To Improving Your Digestion, Health And Wellbeing
PLUS over 80 Delicious Gut-Friendly Recipes

The Essential
Low FODMAP Diet
COOKBOOK

A Quick Start Guide To Relieving the Symptoms of IBS Through Diet
Improve Your Digestion, Health And Wellbeing
PLUS over 75 IBS Friendly Recipes

The Essential
DIABETES DIET
COOKBOOK

A Quick Start Guide To Managing Your Diabetes through Diet
PLUS over 100 Diabetic Friendly Recipes

The
ALKALINE DIET
SOLUTION

A Quick Start Guide To The Alkaline Diet
Lose Weight, Improve Your Health and Feel Great!
PLUS over 90 Alkaline Friendly Recipes

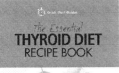

The Essential
THYROID DIET
RECIPE BOOK

A Quick Start Guide To Healing Your Thyroid Through Diet, Lose Weight And Feel Great
With Delicious Thyroid Friendly Recipes

The Essential
SIRT FOOD
DIET RECIPE BOOK

A Quick Start Guide to Cooking on the SIRT Food Diet
Over 100 Easy and Delicious Recipes to Burn Fat, Lose Weight, Get Lean and Feel Great!

What Can I Eat?
ON A
DAIRY FREE
DIET

A Quick Start Guide To Quitting Dairy and Lactose, Lose Weight, Feel Great and Stay Strong!
PLUS 100 Delicious Dairy Free Recipes

LOWER
CHOLESTEROL
DIET

A Quick Start Guide To Lower Cholesterol
Improve Your Health and Feel Great!
PLUS over 100 Delicious Cholesterol Lowering Recipes

THE VEGAN
15 MINUTE
COOKBOOK

Over 100 Simple And Delicious Vegan Recipes For Everyone!

The Essential
ROASTING TIN
COOKBOOK

Over 80 Easy And Delicious One Dish, No-Fuss Oven Recipes

Blood Sugar Diet
Diary

Daily Diary To Track Foods, Weight Loss And Wellbeing On the Blood Sugar Diet

Diabetes Diet
Diary

Daily Diary to Track and Record Diet, Blood Sugar and Wellbeing

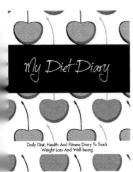

My Diet Diary

Daily Diet, Health And Fitness Diary To Track Weight Loss And Well-being

Low FODMAP
Food Diary

Daily Diary to Track Foods And Symptoms To Beat IBS And Digestive Disorders

Sugar-Free Diet
Diary

Daily Diary For Quitting Sugar, Losing Weight and Feeling Great

FOOD
Diary

Daily Diary To Track Diet And Symptoms To Beat Food Intolerances And Digestive Disorders

Printed in Great Britain
by Amazon

35921519R00062